ENHANCING CROSS-CULTURAL COLLABORATION BETWEEN DOD AND VA

For decades there has been concern about how to improve the collaboration and efficiency between the DoD and VA. In an April 2009 Senate hearing, DoD and VA officials told the committee that, "they have experienced numerous challenges as they worked to jointly develop policies to improve the care, management, and transition of recovering servicemembers."[2] Concerns have radiated from a variety of stakeholders and perspectives. Congress has been intent on reducing duplication and redundancy in order to ease costs, time, and energy by utilizing resources more effectively, and achieve greater unity of effort. The problems confronting interagency collaboration are so complex that they will not yield to single agency or single solutions but rather require robust interventions that are only possible through reform. Even the President is growing frustrated with federal agency inefficiency and redundancy. During a recent speech at the White House, President Obama said, "No business or nonprofit leader would allow this kind of duplication or unnecessary complexity in their operations, so why is it okay in our government? It's not. It has to change."[3] The time is now to initiate interagency reform through policy and program implementation, education and training, interagency assignments, and via the legislative process for enduring change to take hold.

Joint Publication 3-08 (Interagency, Intergovernmental Organization, and Nongovernmental Organization Coordination during Joint Operations) states, "In order for the interagency process to be successful, it should bring together the interests of multiple agencies, departments, and organizations."[4] Although one of the primary areas of interest for both DoD and VA is to care for the same people at different times of their lives, several problems have plagued the two agencies' efforts at successful collaboration. This paper examines interagency collaboration through its historical and current arrangement; reviews current DoD and VA collaboration endeavors; examines existing policies, procedures, and legislation in order to identify factors that have hindered the collaboration process. The paper concludes by offering recommendations to overcome these challenges, to improve efficiency, create better synergy, and achieve greater unity of effort between the two Departments. Improving cross-cultural collaboration between DoD and VA can achieve huge efficiencies while still achieving the end state of caring for the service members, veterans, and their families.

History of the Department of Defense

History offers a means for retrieving and comprehending the past, while in the process, understanding the challenges of our own time. There is no question that our military has an illustrious history. It began in 1775 around the time of the American Revolution when the Army, Navy and Marine Corps were established. On August 7, 1789, the War Department was created, the precursor to what is now the Department of Defense.[5] During this time, each department received its own budget from Congress and reported directly to the President.

World War II saw the importance of joint operations via land, air, and sea. President Harry Truman proposed a plan to create a single cabinet-level department to combine the various departments under one headquarters. After much debate, Congress passed the National Security Act of 1947 which President Truman signed into law on 26 July. The act established the Air Force as a separate military service and created a single organization to oversee the operations of the all the services. James

V. Forrestal was nominated by President Truman to head this organization, originally called the National Military Establishment (NME). The NME ultimately changed to the Department of Defense in 1949. This brought the three services (Army, Navy, and Air Force) under one single civilian secretary to oversee the coordination for the U.S. military; however, the military departments still retained significant autonomy.[6]

In 1949, Congress amended the National Security Act to create the current Department of Defense structure that shifted more power to the Secretary of Defense (SecDef). The amendment withdrew cabinet-level status from the three service Secretaries and provided broader power to the SecDef to directly manage the armed forces rather than just coordinate their activities.

The current chain of command now runs from the President (i.e. The Commander-in-Chief) through the SecDef to the Secretaries of the military departments when dealing with force structure, and to the combatant commanders (COCOMs) for operational matters. The Chairman of the Joint Chiefs of Staff serves as the principle military adviser to the President and the SecDef. The Joint Chiefs of Staff consists of: the Chairman, Vice Chairman, Chief of Staff of the Army, Chief of Naval Operations, Chief of Staff of the Air Force, Commandant of the Marine Corps, and the Chief of the National Guard Bureau.[7]

History of the Veterans Affairs

In 1775, as a recruiting tool for the Continental Army, the Continental Congress passed the first national veterans' pension law, which granted half-pay for life for loss of a limb or other "serious" disability. Unfortunately, there was no money to fund the program, and its actual implementation was left up to the individual states. With the end of the war and the subsequent approval of the U.S. Constitution, the first Congress assumed responsibility for paying veterans' benefits. The first Federal Veterans law was passed in 1789; it continued the pension law previously passed by the Continental Congress.[8]

Benefits for Civil War veterans were restricted to those veterans who had fought on the Union side. Confederate soldiers were not legally recognized as "veterans" until 1958. After the Civil War, there were no new pension programs for a number of years. Specifically, there were no new benefits programs for veterans of the Spanish-American War or the Philippine Insurrection. In 1912, the Sherwood Act granted an automatic pension at age 62 to all veterans, including Mexican War and (Union) Civil War Veterans.[9]

In 1812, Veterans homes for medical care were first established with the Naval Home in Philadelphia. In 1853 and 1855, the Soldiers Home and St. Elizabeth's Hospital followed in Washington, DC. In 1866, Congress established the National Homes for Disabled Volunteer Soldiers. Initially, they only provided domiciliary services plus incidental medical care for disabled and indigent Union veterans. The quality of medical care at these homes improved until it was comparable to hospital care of that day. In 1862, the National Cemetery System was established to provide burial for the Union soldiers. In 1873, the scope of the National Cemetery System was enlarged to provide for burial for all honorably discharged Union veterans.[10]

In 1914, a Bureau of War Risk Insurance was established under the Treasury Department, to insure American ships and their cargo against the dangers of carrying war materials to the Allies. When the United States entered World War I in 1917, the

Bureau of War Risk Insurance was assigned the additional tasks of providing life insurance for American soldiers and administering veterans' and survivors' benefits after the war.[11] In 1921, the Veterans Bureau was established as an independent agency to consolidate all benefits for World War I veterans (i.e. life insurance, disability and death compensation, vocational rehabilitation, and medical care) under one agency. The Bureau of Pensions and the National Homes for Disabled Volunteer Soldiers continued to operate independently and handled benefits and care for veterans of previous wars and their survivors.[12]

On July 21, 1930, the Veterans Administration (VA) was established by merging the Veterans Bureau, the Bureau of Pensions, and the National Homes for Disabled Volunteer Soldiers, thus bringing all veterans' benefits programs under the jurisdiction of a single agency. The National Cemetery System remained under the jurisdiction of the War Department.[13] After World War II, the Veterans Administration grew to become the largest non-cabinet agency in the Federal Government. In 1973, the Army transferred control of the National Cemetery System to VA. The only exception was Arlington National Cemetery and the Soldiers' Home National Cemetery.[14]

On March 15, 1989, the Veterans Administration changed its name to the U.S. Department of Veterans Affairs, finally becoming a cabinet-level agency. The Administrator of Veterans Affairs became the Secretary of Veterans Affairs. The new agency was composed of three primary sub-agencies: the Veterans Benefits Administration (VBA), the Veterans Health Administration (VHA), and the National Cemetery Administration (NCA), each lead by an Under Secretary.[15] The Department of

Veterans Affairs is the second-largest agency in the Federal Government, second in size only to the Department of Defense.

Historical Progress of the Interagency - How Did We Get Here?

There are considerable challenges in achieving effective interagency collaboration. Such problems include: leadership, cultural barriers, priorities, unity of effort, unity of command, conflicting goals and missions, and unequal decision-making authority. While there is no commonly accepted definition for collaboration, for the purpose of this paper we will use the definition given by Eugene Bardach, "Any joint activity by two or more agencies that is intended to increase public value by their working together rather than separately."[16] For decades there has been extensive and constant pressure to achieve more coordination between government agencies. A good start would be to review the historical development of the interagency.

Although the roots of interagency collaboration are found in the constitution, the modern approach did not occur until 1947. Following the end of World War II, President Truman sent a message to Congress recommending major legislative change to better face the challenges of the future. In his 1947 State of the Union address, President Truman said, "There is one certain way by which we can cut costs and at the same time enhance our national security. That is by the establishment of a single Department of National Defense."[17] On July 26, 1947, The *National Security Act of 1947*, created the military we see today by establishing the U.S. Air Force, unifying the services under a single cabinet-level secretary named the Secretary of Defense (SecDef). It also created the Central Intelligence Agency (CIA) and the National Security Council (NSC).[18] The *National Security Act of 1947* was extremely significant during its time as it attained a higher degree of integration allowing the U.S. military "to operate as one of the greatest fighting forces ever assembled."[19]

Even with such drastic legislative change, it was clear to many in Congress and the military that the *National Security Act of 1947* did little to help with inter-service collaboration and cultural rivalries. The military failure in Vietnam, the disastrous American hostage rescue attempt in Iran, and the Marine barracks bombing in Beirut illustrated the weakness of joint military operations, unity of command, and unity of effort.[20] The Goldwater-Nichols Department of Defense Reorganization Act (GNA) of 1986 attempted to strengthen these shortcomings. It strengthened civilian control of the military, increased the powers of the Chairman of the Joint Chiefs of Staff (CJCS), restructured the military chain of command which now runs from the President, through the SecDef, to the COCOMs, and mandated the establishment of a joint officer management system.[21] Although the role of the CJCS and the COCOMs were enhanced, and the Service Chiefs have clear responsibility to man, train, and equip their force, there still lacked clear guidance on the role of the Service Secretaries. A July 2005 report by the Center for Strategic and International Studies stated, "Although the Secretary's formal authority is unquestioned, the actual degree of control and influence of any particular Secretary over the Pentagon has varied widely, depending on the Secretary, his most senior military interlocutors, and the issues at stake."[22]

GNA reform clearly facilitated a successful Desert Storm operation in 1991, Kosovo operations in 1999, and the decisive invasion of Iraq in 2003 that toppled Saddam Hussein.[23] The military has a much more capable joint force now due to the GNA. But clearly more work was needed. Failures in interagency collaboration, leadership, unity of command, and unity of effort were evident in the sluggish response to the 9/11 attacks. The U.S. government did not have a strong interagency system in place to plan, coordinate, synchronize, and execute decisive action against the enemy. The 9/11 Commission Report gives details to some of the factors that contributed to the ineffective reaction to the attacks. The report describes that many government agencies still relied on Cold War era, stove-pipe systems that did not allow for cross-talk and coordination across agencies.[24] Hurricane Katrina is another prime example of poor interagency collaboration. In the bipartisan committee report to investigate the preparation for and response to Hurricane Katrina, the committee said, "If 9/11 was a failure of imagination, then Katrina was a failure of initiative. It was a failure of leadership."[25] The report also notes that the lack of unity of effort, unity of command, communication, and interagency cultural bias played a major role in the handling of Katrina.

The complexity and inherent risk associated with unity of effort are abundant, especially when dealing with multiple government agencies. As the two largest government agencies, DoD and VA have similar challenges but also many of the same interests. One primary area of interest is to care for the same people, only at different times of their lives. The partnership between the DoD and VA is starting to take shape after decades of congressional interest. The partnership began in April 1982 when Congress signed *Public Law 97-174*, S.266, *Veterans Administration and Department of Defense Health Resources Sharing and Emergency Operations Act*, in order to advance DoD and VA sharing.[26] The intent of the act was a step in the right direction. According to the TRICARE Management Activity, this act has "resulted in over 200 sharing agreements and eight joint ventures covering a wide range of services such as medical/surgical, traumatic brain injury, blind rehabilitation, spinal cord injury, and physical examinations. The intent of resource sharing is to promote cost-effective use of federal healthcare resources by minimizing duplication and underuse of healthcare resources while benefiting both VA and DoD beneficiaries."[27]

Congress as well as senior DoD and VA leadership understood that more needed to be done to improve healthcare and benefits delivery to our nation's veterans. On November 24, 2003, Congress passed the *National Defense Authorization Act* (NDAA) for FY2004, *Public Law 108-136*, section 583, and is codified in title 38, United States Code, Section 320.[28] It created the DoD/VA Joint Executive Committee (JEC) co-chaired by the Deputy Secretary (DepSec) of Veterans Affairs (VA) and the Under Secretary of Defense (USD) for Personnel and Readiness (P&R).[29] The primary mission of the JEC is to ensure VA and DoD deliver high quality, economic health care, and benefits services to eligible active duty and veterans beneficiaries.[30] The JEC promotes an unprecedented level of cooperation between DoD and VA as they work to remove the cultural barriers and address the operational and strategic challenges in caring for veterans. Additionally, the JEC: (1) oversees the development and implementation of the VA/DoD Joint Strategic Plan (JSP); (2) prepares the Annual Report to Secretaries and Congress; (3) identifies opportunities to enhance mutually beneficial services and resources; and (4) oversees its three sub-councils, the Health Executive Council (HEC), the Benefits Executive Council (BEC), and the Interagency Program Office (IPO).[31] Figure 1 depicts the JEC organizational structure. The JSP is, "the primary source document that conveys to the Secretaries of the Departments the

JEC's recommendations for the strategic direction of joint coordination and sharing efforts between the two Departments."[32] The HEC, BEC, and IPO supervise the development and implementation of the JSP objectives and milestones that fall under their purview while the respective co-chairs provide status updates to the JEC.

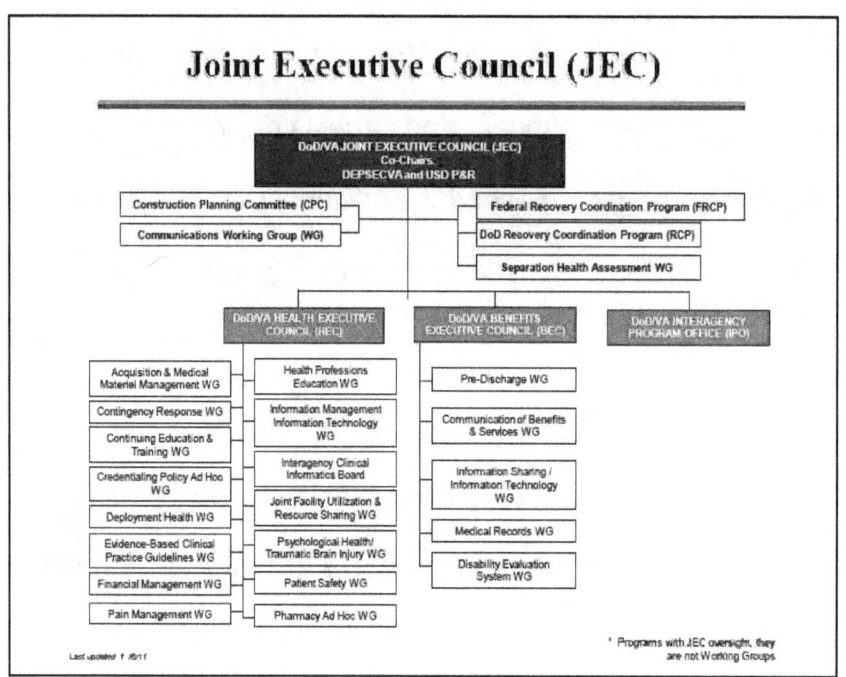

Figure 1[33]

A push for greater collaboration between the two Departments came with the *National Defense Authorization Act for Fiscal Year 2008* (NDAA 2008) requiring DoD and VA, "to jointly develop and implement a comprehensive policy on improvements to the care, management, and transition of recovering Service Members."[34] Prior to the *NDAA 2008*, the Washington Post published a series of damaging articles about the problems at Walter Reed in February 2007. This prompted President Bush on March 6, 2007, to establish *The President's Commission on Care for America's Returning Wounded Warriors*, also known as the *Dole-Shalala Commission*, to provide a comprehensive review of the care provided to American's returning in support of the Global War on Terror.[35]

On May 3, 2007, Secretary of Defense Robert Gates asked Deputy Secretary of Defense Gordon England to convene a Senior Oversight Committee (SOC) with the VA to deliver a seamless continuum of healthcare and benefits services to Wounded, Ill, and Injured (WII) service members and their families in transition to continued military service or veterans status.[36] The SOC was co-chaired by the Deputy Secretaries of DoD and VA. It was meant to serve as a temporary body formed to implement quick new initiatives to care for WII. The SOC was organized into eight subordinate Lines of Action (LoAs), each co-led by representatives from VA and DoD; and the Overarching Integrated Product Team (OIPT), a committee comprised of the LOA co-chairs and co-chaired by the VA's Under Secretary for Benefits and DoD's Principal Deputy USD (P&R). The OIPT receives guidance from and reports back to the SOC. It supervises, coordinates, and directs the work of the LoAs to address the needs of the WII.[37] Depicted in Figure 2 is the organizational structure for the SOC and LoAs. Collectively, the JEC and SOC address the countless recommendations and mandates from various commissions and legislation to achieve a seamless transition of service members to veteran status.

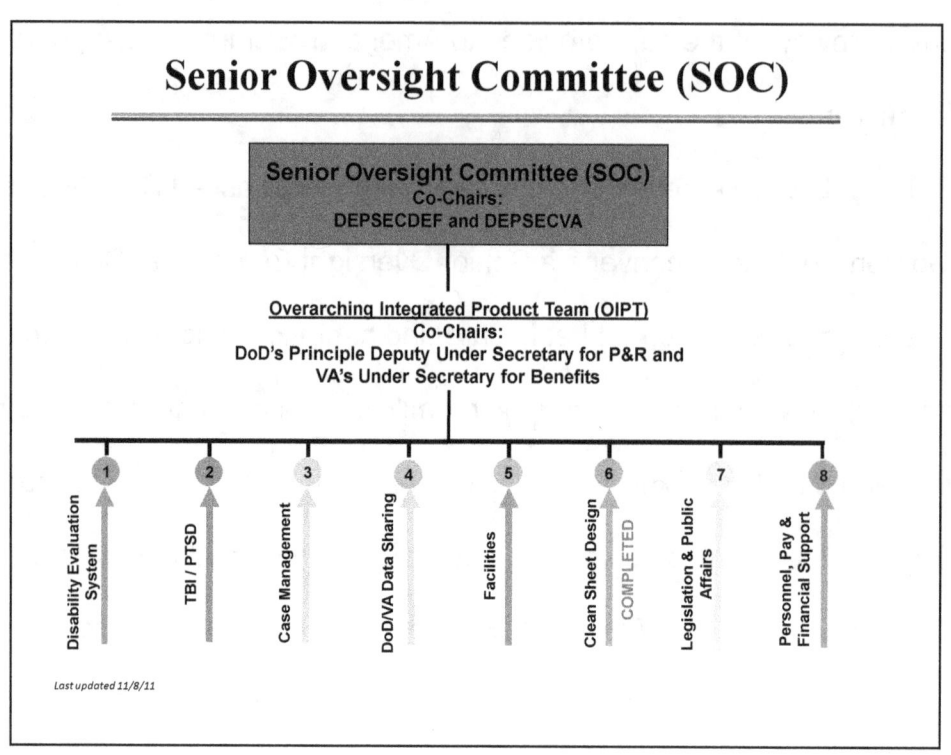

Figure 2[38]

Another illustration of DoD and VA collaboration that resulted from the *Dole-Shalala Commission* was the creation of the Federal Recovery Coordination Program (FRCP). On October 30, 2007, a joint DoD and VA Memorandum of Understanding (MOU) was signed, establishing the FRCP.[39] The FRCP was established, "to assist severely wounded, ill, and injured Operation Enduring Freedom (OEF) and Operation Iraqi Freedom (OIF) service members, veterans, and their families with access to care and benefits provided through DoD, VA, other federal agencies, states, and the private sector."[40] The FRCP is a joint DoD and VA program to assist WII service members and veterans not likely to return to active duty.[41] An assigned care coordinator, with a clinical background, helps the service member and family navigate through a myriad of obstacles ranging from income support, vocational rehabilitation, health care, and education to name a few. Although the program was jointly created, it is managed by

12

the VA and the care coordinators are VA employees. It is intended to serve as the single point of contact among a myriad of case managers of DoD, VA, and other government and private care coordination and case management programs.[42]

The DoD has a separate program called the Recovery Coordination Program (RCP) established by *Public Law 110-181, NDAA 2008*, Title XVI Sec. 1611 (Comprehensive Policy on Improvements to Care, Management, and Transition of Recovering Service Members).[43] It is a DoD program that uses non-clinical care coordinators to oversee and assist the service member through the entire spectrum of care, management, transition, and rehabilitation services available from the Federal Government, including services provided by the DoD, VA, Department of Labor, and the Social Security Administration.[44] While the RCP resides under the DoD's Office of Wounded Warrior Care and Transition Policy, each service has implemented separate programs to manage their individual warriors. According to the October 6, 2011 GAO report, "The FRCP and RCP are two of at least a dozen DoD and VA programs that provide care coordination and case management services to recovering servicemembers, veterans, and their families."[45]

Since 2000, DoD and VA have electronically shared information. The initial sharing was primarily supporting personnel and administrative needs, followed by periodic sharing necessary for continuity of care and benefits administration. Faced with a mutual need to modernize the legacy Electronic Health Record (EHR) systems and problems in sharing health care information, Congress ordered DoD and VA to create the Interagency Program Office (IPO) in Sec. 1635, *NDAA 2008*.[46] The purpose of the IPO is to, "(1) act as a single point of accountability for the Department of

Defense and the Department of Veterans Affairs in the rapid development and implementation of electronic health record systems or capabilities that allow for full interoperability of personal health care information between the Department of Defense and the Department of Veterans Affairs and (2) To accelerate the exchange of health care information between the Department of Defense and the Department of Veterans Affairs in order to support the delivery of health care by both Departments."[47] Although the act was signed in 2008, it took several years to get the IPO to Full Operational Capability (FOC). According to a Federal Times article, "bureaucratic fighting among its sponsoring departments, a lack of leadership and acute understaffing" have delayed the IPO.[48] A new charter signed on October 27, 2011 by VA Deputy Secretary Scott Gould and Deputy Secretary of Defense William Lynn outlines the office's mission, structure, and responsibilities, which include the creation of the Virtual Lifetime Electronic Record (VLER).[49] The VLER is envisioned to be a single access point for service members' and veterans' medical information throughout their lifetime. The IPO is led by a DoD Senior Executive Service (SES) Director and a VA SES Deputy Director. They receive direction, supervision, and control from the Department Secretaries and recommendations from the IPO Advisory Board who is co-chaired by the respective Chief Information Officers (CIOs). To add a little confusion to the mix, the IPO also receives guidance from the JEC.

The final collaboration effort discussed in this paper is the Captain James A. Lovell Federal Health Care Center (FHCC). The *NDAA 2010* authorized the DoD and VA to establish a five-year demonstration project integrating the North Chicago VA Medical Center and the Naval Health Clinic Great Lakes.[50] The FHCC is named in honor of retired U.S. Naval officer and Illinois resident, Captain James A. Lovell, who

was an astronaut on Apollo 13. The joint facility serves the medical needs of active duty

service members, veterans, and TRICARE beneficiaries around the Northern Illinois

and Southern Wisconsin area. It is considered a ground-breaking, fully integrated,

federal health care center with a single combined VA and Navy mission. It offers a full

spectrum of services, including ambulatory care, surgery, mental health services,

pharmacy, nursing care, dental services, and fleet medicine.[51] Nowhere else in the

country will you find such a joint relationship between the DoD and VA. Unlike other

joint venture facilities, the *NDAA 2010* established a single funding source called the

Joint DoD and VA Medical Facility Demonstration Fund.[52] Monies are transferred into

the joint fund from their respective appropriations thus allowing easier access. The

leadership and workforce remain directly accountable to their individual departments;

however, the FHCC reports to the HEC for direction and guidance. This revolutionary

partnership promises to provide comprehensive, patient centered care to veterans while

still maintaining the highest level of readiness for sailors and service members.

Why the Challenges?

While there have been some positive collaboration between DoD and VA, more

remains to be done, especially with the current political and economic environment.[53]

After over a decade of war, cultural barriers, inadequate oversight and accountability,

insufficient program and policy implementation, and bureaucratic turmoil continue to

impede the goal of caring for service members, veterans, and their families. The only

two entities within DoD and VA that can effectively ensure both departments are

working in harmony vice discord are the Senior Oversight Committee (SOC) and Joint

Executive Committee (JEC). The problem is that there is no true arbitrator when there is disagreement, it lacks unity of effort, and there is duplication within the two bodies. The impetus for the SOC was politically driven to address shortcomings in the delivery of medical care, disability processing, and transition activities in response to the Walter Reed incident. In short, it was the tactical solution to streamline, deconflict, and expedite services in support of WII service members, veterans, and their families. The JEC was designed to create efficiencies in health care and resource sharing. Consequently, the JEC's focus is on strategic planning, infrastructure, logistics, procurement, and is designed to be more long-term focused. With a fully operational capable forum in the JEC already established to handle DoD and VA issues, was the SOC structure ever needed? Several members of the SOC have said they were never certain as to the SOC's decision-making authority.[54] Others complained that unlike the JEC, there were no clear objectives and goals (i.e. metrics) established in the SOC.[55] As stated earlier, the JEC prepares the JSP with clear objectives and milestones where the SOC does not. Proponents for the SOC argue that it has been successful largely due to the ranks of members, primarily uniformed service members. In their 2011 Annual Report, the DoD *Recovering Warrior Task Force* (RWTF) recommended to, "consolidate the SOC functions into the JEC"[56] due to the concerns listed above.

The final decision to combine the SOC functions into the JEC was cemented during a DoD/VA Executive Session in January 2012. However, with the White House, Congress, and the American public significantly engaged in wounded, ill, and injured issues, is this the right time to eliminate the SOC forum? Does the new JEC solve the problem with effective and efficient accountability and oversight of key issues? One thing is certain, the SOC and JEC consolidation will limit time spent on WII issues, specifically the Integrated Disability Evaluation System (IDES). In FY11, the SOC met for a total of 10.75 hours.[57] Out of the 10.75 hours, 4.67 hours or 44% of the time was spent on IDES related issues.[58] With a consolidated JEC forum and the frequency and duration of the meetings set at bi-monthly and two hours, how can DoD and VA provide effective oversight of all the key issues? To mitigate some of the concerns relating to WII issues, the new JEC structure established the Wounded, Ill, and Injured Committee (WIIC) to oversee and monitor the execution of mandates, recommendations, and taskings related to WII service members and veterans. The WIIC will effectively be the primary advisor to the JEC on all WII issues and report directly to the JEC co-chairs. Only time will tell if this mitigation strategy works.

The DoD's RCP and VA's FRCP is a prime example of inefficient and ineffective policy, legislation, and duplication. Although both DoD and VA recognize that the two programs are complimentary and not redundant programs, Congress requested an analysis of potential options for integrating the FRCP and RCP under a single umbrella.[59] An October 6, 2011 GAO report states, "The two Departments have made prior attempts to jointly develop options for improved collaboration and potential integration of the FRCP and RCP. Despite these efforts, no final decisions to revamp, merge, or eliminate programs have been agreed upon."[60] The two programs are interconnected and are sometimes seen as fulfilling the same roles and responsibilities in their respective agencies. While both the DoD and VA care coordination programs pride themselves as being joint, the truth of the matter is both are managed and operated in conflicting manners. The lack of collaboration and coordination between

17

DoD and VA to better integrate the FRCP and RCP efforts will worsen according to the GAO report.[61] The two Departments have yet to fix their policy and procedures since the inception of the FRCP and RCP, and are not likely to do so without legislative reform. The current FRCP and RCP policies and procedures are confusing to say the least. A "jointly" developed care coordination program to care, manage, and transition recovering warriors did not occur. What we have today is a complicated, service unique, fragmented service care coordination programs that are different in each of the military departments. Cultural bias and interagency bureaucracies too often end up putting organizational interest in front of those of the wounded warriors and their families.

Leadership is the process of influencing people by providing purpose, direction, and motivation while operating to accomplish the mission and improving the organization.[62] Successful collaboration is directly related to the cooperation, participation, and mutual engagement of senior leaders on both sides of the table. During several joint DoD and VA workgroup meetings, DoD leadership has repeatedly questioned the need for senior leader involvement in the SOC and JEC. Since the summer of 2011, DoD has sent the USD (P&R) to SOC meetings instead of the Deputy Secretary of Defense (DepSecDef). Additionally, unlike the SOC where the co-chairs were the Deputy Secretaries of DoD and VA, the new JEC forum will be co-chaired by the VA DepSec and the USD (P&R). What are the optics of relegating the DoD co-chair duties to the USD (P&R) during a time of war? The need still exists for the Deputy Secretaries to reinforce the importance of DoD and VA collaboration and to motivate subordinate leadership. The absence of DoD senior leadership diminishes command emphasis, visibility, and momentum on key issues. With the DepSec VA co-chairing the JEC, it could also be perceived that VA is attempting to dominate the agenda and execution of joint meetings. The partnership begins to breakdown when leadership sets the wrong tone.

Leadership that supports the elements of unity of effort is a must. Probably as significant as leadership, is that the concept of collaboration must become ingrained in the culture of an organization. Sunil B. Desai writes, "With a strong interagency culture, individuals within the interagency community would be far more likely to cooperate to achieve broader interagency goals even when those goals are not fully in line with their own agency's goals."[63] There's no question that the cultures of the two Departments are very different. This fact was evident when senior leaders within DoD said during a RWTF meeting on February 21, 2012, that the 21 recommendation made by the congressionally mandated task force to improve warrior care would be difficult, if not impossible, to implement due to the cultural differences.[64] The number one recommendation by the task force was to adopt common standards and nomenclature for wounded warrior programs and policies. The Principle Director of DoD's Wounded Warrior Care and Transition Policy stated a change in nomenclature sounds simple but it would be difficult to implement. He stated, "I love the idea of consistency; I wish we could all just go with lance corporal and corporal, ranks I've already memorized. Quite frankly, I don't think we are going to get there."[65] There is no question that the lack of common language and nomenclature can damage interagency collaboration. Public confusion and anger can occur when different nomenclature is used for recovering warriors, programs, and policies from different agencies supposedly working together in a coordinated fashion.[66]

Historically, government agencies are structured in a vertical stovepipe where horizontal planning, coordination, and synchronization are sometimes hindered. Former Vice Chairman of the Joint Chiefs of Staff General Peter Pace emphasized this during a speech, saying, "our government goes back into its stovepipes for execution."[67] It makes staff access to the SOC and JEC senior leadership almost impossible. Unlike the VA staff that has unrestricted access to the DepSecVA, the DoD staff has limited access to the USD (P&R) and almost no access to the DepSecDef due to its siloed structure. The VA has a meticulous process for preparing the VA senior leadership for the SOC and JEC meetings. VA subject matter experts (SMEs) and support staff routinely brief VA senior leadership. This normal battle rhythm allows time for obtaining leadership guidance and intent. In comparison, DoD does not have a process to pre-brief their senior leaders nor do they invite their SMEs.

Establishment of the SOC and JEC resulted in improved interagency coordination and increased accountability to the Secretaries; however, it failed to address the decision-making authority and resources at the staff level. Why would any staff put forth any resources, personnel and energy behind an initiative if it were perceived that their department's leadership would not support it in the long run? Additionally, they may not share information because doing so may be outside their department's culture or because of political concerns, such as revealing potential vulnerabilities with that organization. This only aggravates the situation and creates an environment where unity of effort cannot rise above the lack in unity of command.

Currently DoD and VA have two separate support offices that work collaboration issues on a daily basis. However, since the summer of 2011, the VA staff has routinely taken the lead in developing and editing the SOC and JEC guidance, VA/DoD Annual Report, and the VA/DoD Joint Strategic Plan (JSP). Because of the familiarity of the two agencies and some retired service members working in the VA support staff office, many of the systems are institutionalized and standard business practices allow for mutually supporting efforts.

The VA mitigated some of the risks associated with the lack of DoD collaboration by creating the VA/DoD Collaboration Service in October 2008 under the Assistant Secretary for Policy and Planning (OPP). Their mission is to facilitate the development of joint policies and programs between the two services.[68] Additionally, it provides oversight for the implementation of joint VA/DoD programs and policies as they relate to activities of the JEC.[69] The DoD created a similar office buried in the DoD's Office of Wounded Warrior Care and Transition Policy (WWCTP) Office in early 2009. Their mission is ensuring equitable, consistent, high-quality support and service for wounded warriors and their families, as well as transitioning members of the Armed Forces, through effective outreach, interagency collaboration, policy and program oversight.[70] According to a recent *Army Times* article, the WWCTP office is cutting about 40 percent of their contracted staff.[71] These cuts will undoubtedly hurt their efforts to ensure that our wounded warrior and their families are cared for within the DoD system but also impede the delicate task of interagency collaboration and decision-making.

Building a collaborative team requires a well trained, adaptable, and agile workforce with the requisite skills and experience to integrate their agencies assorted capabilities and resources to accomplish the mission. However, some federal government agencies lack the personnel capacity to accomplish this endeavor, and DoD and VA are no exceptions. In the absence of adequate personnel capacity, some government agencies have relied on contractors to fill the roles that traditionally have been performed by federal employees. As stated earlier, contractors primarily filled DoD's interagency collaboration office. When the federal government began downsizing earlier this year, nearly 40% of the DoD's collaboration staff was cut. While the use of contractors to support day-to-day operations in the federal government is not new, the actual numbers of contractors and the work they perform have skyrocketed since 9/11.[72] Contractors provide the federal agencies certain benefits such as flexibility and the ability to fill an immediate requirement. However, there are many risks associated with hiring contractors, notably, higher cost and conflicts of interest. A recent study uncovered that a computer engineer working for the federal government was paid an average of $268,653, while the government worker in the same field made $136,456.[73] Contractors working in the human resources management field were paid an average of $228,488, twice the $111,711 that was paid in-house.[74] In February 2012, the VA abruptly terminated its first major contract to create software for the joint DoD and VA integrated Electronic Health Record (iEHR) due to a conflict of interest issue.[75]

There have been a myriad of lessons learned in the creation of the iEHR, in both the IPO and FHCC organization, but there is no single repository to collect, analyze, and disseminate lessons and best practices for future joint endeavors. The DoD and VA have two of the nation's largest health care systems.[76] For the past decade or so, the DoD and VA have built and used two separate Electronic Health Record (EHR) systems to support over 9.6 million active duty service members and their beneficiaries, and six million veterans with estimated annual costs of about $49 billion and $48 billion, respectively.[77] The DoD uses the Armed Forces Health Longitudinal Technology Application (AHLTA) and the VA uses the Veterans Health Information System and Technology Architecture (VistA) system. Faced with a mutual need to modernize the legacy EHR systems, in May 2011, Defense Secretary Robert Gates and VA Secretary Eric Shinseki formally agreed to develop a joint EHR that will not only improve DoD and VA information sharing but also be the foundation for sharing electronic health information nationally.[78] Furthermore, DoD and VA began working on the VLER that is anticipated to facilitate the sharing of, "both administrative (i.e. personnel and benefits) and medical information for service members and veterans."[79] VLER is intended to expand the departments' information sharing by enabling access to private sector organizations and other federal agencies such as the Social Security Administration.[80] However, a February 2011 GAO report cited concerns in the areas of: strategic planning, enterprise architecture, and investment management when planning and implementing joint IT solutions. This resulted in both DoD's and VA's decision to focus on developing separate EHR systems that ultimately affected the initial IT capability at the FHCC in North Chicago.[81]

There have been some improvements with regard to overall IT management between the two Departments with the renewed emphasis in the IPO. Additionally, the FHCC has had both DoD and VA personnel working side-by-side providing seamless care to active duty service members, veterans, retirees, and their family members in a fully integrated medical facility for over a year. History has proven that merely collecting such lessons and best practices, without incorporating those lessons into current and future endeavors, completely negates learning and destines the DoD and VA to repeat mistakes of the past.

Overcoming These Challenges – Toward a Better Future

There are a several recommendations that emerge to improve cross-cultural collaboration between DoD and VA. These recommendations would reshape how the two Departments operate and also create the necessary capacity to accomplish any mission.

Rename the Joint Executive Committee (JEC)

There is no replacement for an active and involved Congress. Only Congress has the political muscle necessary to penetrate the bureaucratic friction. However, congressional legislation creates significant challenges especially when dealing with the two largest government agencies. But to significantly improve the partnership between DoD and VA, the newly formed JEC body needs reform. The recommendation below presents "a way" to implement change but would ultimately require congressional action. The first step is to amend and modify section 320, title 38, Unites States Code by renaming the JEC and establish the VA/DoD Senior Executive Council (SEC).

Removing all references to the JEC allows for a fresh start, eliminating any negative connotations that were associated with the SOC or JEC. Legislative action would be required because as stated earlier, law mandates the JEC. The SEC, as did the JEC and SOC, would incorporate the high level of success and rigorous oversight with the broader scope and more structured reporting and tracking requirements of the

JEC. As a standing permanent body, the SEC would provide the administration, Congress, and other stakeholders with a single access point for all matters having to do with coordination and collaboration between DoD and VA.

Reform Membership in the Senior Executive Council (SEC)

The SOC was successful because it had the capability to develop and implement a rapid response to an identified issue or concern because it was co-chaired by the Deputy Secretaries of DoD and VA. Therefore, the co-chairs of the SEC would be the Deputy Secretaries of the two Departments (the same as the old SOC structure). At a minimum, members would include for DoD: the Under Secretary of Defense for Personnel and Readiness; Chief Information Officer; the Secretaries of the military services; the Chairman or Vice Chairman of the Joint Chiefs of Staff; and the Chiefs or Vice Chiefs of Staff of the military services. For VA, the members include: the Under Secretaries of Veterans Affairs for Health and Benefits; and the Assistant Secretary for Information and Technology.

To maximize the potential for real transformation and to limit the natural tendency for cultural bias and stove-piping, it is important that the structure of the new SEC include an arbitrator - a member with no ties, cultural bias, or influence from either DoD or VA. Although the two Departments agree on many issues, there are some issues that required an intermediary when there is discord. A member from the Office of Management and Budget (OMB) would squelch such discord. The OMB is a cabinet-level office, and is the largest office within the Executive Office of the President of the United States. The primary mission of the OMB is to help formulate the President's spending plans; evaluate the effectiveness of agency programs, policies, and procedures; assess competing funding demands among agencies; and sets funding priorities.[82] Additionally, the OMB ensures that agency reports, rules, testimony, and proposed legislation are consistent with the President's budget and with administration policies.[83]

Establish an Interagency Support Staff (ISS)

If unity of effort does not come from senior leadership, any initiatives to create unity of effort at the subordinate agencies and among its staff will collapse. Unity of effort cannot be overstated as Michele Flournoy emphasized the importance of "unity of effort" in her testimony before Congress, noting: "unity of effort across the U.S. government is not just about being more efficient or even more effective in operations. It can determine whether the United States succeeds or fails in a given intervention."[84] To improve collaboration and unity of effort at the supporting staff level, a solution is to establish a truly joint staff office called the DoD/VA Interagency Support Staff (ISS) co-located under one roof. The office would be headed by a Senior Executive Service (SES) director and deputy director and would serve a 3-4 year term. The position of the director and deputy director would alternate between the DoD and VA.

As mentioned earlier, the two Departments have separate support staffs. There are time when they become unsynchronized working on the same issue. The new staff office will prepare and coordinate between the departments required actions, reports, and testimony; track implementation of recommendations and mandates; and carry out such responsibilities, duties, and activities as determined by the SEC co-chairs. The ISS office will consist of an equal number of DoD and VA employees ranging from General Schedule (GS) 12-14. One DoD and VA staff member will be assigned to a particular workgroup responsible for coordinating, synchronizing, and monitoring the necessary actions to push paperwork through their respective agency. Co-location is important as it affords the staff opportunities for face-to-face interaction, interagency understanding, and relationship building over time. Relationship building is critical to the successful collaboration. Co-location, while difficult to implement, may provide a good long-term approach to interagency integration.

Create the Center for Interagency Lessons Learned (CILL)

The military Services have mature lessons learned programs established. They have been collecting and analyzing lessons and best practices from the field for years. The U.S. Army has an excellent knowledge management/best practice office called the Center for Army Lessons Learned (CALL) located at Fort Leavenworth, KS. CALL was established after Operation Urgent Fury (Grenada) in 1983.[85] Operation Urgent Fury showed that the Army and other services did not have a formal system in place to collect, organize, analyze, and disseminate knowledge (i.e. lessons learned) related to field operations and exercises.[86] Operation Iraqi Freedom (OIF) and Operation Enduring Freedom (OEF) allowed the Army to apply and refine the CALL system. The dynamic operational environment and rapidly changing enemy tactics, techniques, and procedures make knowledge management essential to units. To survive and defeat the enemy, one must learn as quickly as the situation changes making CALL an invaluable asset.

Unfortunately, the DoD and VA does not have a joint lessons learned capability to examine and adopt lessons learned and best practices from the iEHR, VLER, FHCC, IPO, and other joint projects. A permanent solution would be for Congress to create the

27

Center for Interagency Lessons Learned (CILL) - a joint DoD and VA best practice/knowledge management center. The purpose of the CILL would be to collect, organize, analyze, and disseminate lessons learned and best practices from joint ventures and projects like the iEHR, VLER, FHCC and IPO. If an office like the CILL existed previously, the FHCC would have known that receiving direction from a single entity is better than a "complex, duplicative, two-department solution" when establishing a joint DoD and VA healthcare center.[87] Such an office could also give DoD and VA an opportunity to assist and influence the larger civilian healthcare community. In the end, to develop a culture of collaboration within an organization, it must become a "learning organization" with a capacity to take risks, disagree, make mistakes, and learn from those mistakes. There could be a natural tendency by one or both the services not to "look bad" under the spotlight. However, just as the Services have done with respect to their lessons learned organizations, DoD and VA senior leadership must stress that the new office is no way evaluating the performance of an individual or section but only attempting to improve effectiveness and efficiency of the organization. Effective knowledge management only enhances the shared understanding of an organization. The CILL will build trust within the two agencies, generate a shared understanding, and the people and organization will grow.

Establish the Interagency Recovery Care Coordination (IRCC) Office

Army Field Manual 3-0 (Operations) defines unity of command as, "For every objective, ensure unity of effort under one responsible commander."[88] Unity of command is a principle of war that ensures accountability and responsibility. By this definition, one person has ultimate responsibility for the mission and any other actions under his/her purview. It is difficult, if not impossible, to achieve unity of command when dealing with government agencies, many with separate budgets, missions, and oversight bodies. A more realistic effort for all stakeholders involved would be to achieve unity of effort. It is apparent that the FRCP and RCP continue to experience considerable challenges in areas such as policy, funding, and program management. Furthermore, there is considerable duplication and overlap between the two programs with regard to mission and patient population. Coordination problems impede the efficiencies and effectiveness that can be made through mutual policy making and execution by agencies responsible for a common policy. Competition or confusion over control or misinterpretation of a policy can lead to conflict among services and the development of parallel and redundant systems. This was apparent when Chairwoman Ann Buerkle commented to a senior DoD official during a hearing on the Federal Recovery Coordination Program stating, "It seems to me now 4 years after this program started that you would have policy and then you would work through that policy. And when VA says we are not getting referrals quickly enough, you would alter that policy and this would be a moving, developing policy. But, it seems like we do not have that."[89] To overcome this challenge, a recommendation is to terminate FRCP and amend *Public Law 110-181, NDAA 2008*, Title XVI Sec. 1611 (Comprehensive Policy on Improvements to Care, Management, and Transition of Recovering Service Members) to form a single, joint Interagency Recovery Care Coordination (IRCC) office.

The FRCP was a great initiative by VA and DoD considering the findings by the *Dole-Shalala Commission.* Since then, the services are more capable of caring for their own WII service members but still require help transitioning and tracking "severely"

29

wounded, ill and injured service members to veteran status. Therefore the IRCC office will retain the FRCP care coordinators, with a clinical background, to assist in this endeavor. The new IRCC will integrate the responsibilities of both the FRCP and RCP and eliminate the duplication. The office would be headed by a SES director and deputy director. The position of the director and deputy director could alternate between the DoD and VA every three to four years. Additionally, establish a single line of accounting to fund anything to do with joint DoD and VA care coordination management. Currently, there is no mechanism to ensure sufficient resources are applied to this effort. Therefore, it could be perceived that one agency is putting more energy and resources behind its program than the other. Legislative change would be required because as stated earlier, law mandates the RCP. As a joint office, the IRCC would provide the administration, Congress, and other stockholders with a single access point for all matters to do with DoD and VA care coordination. It will ultimately simplify the process, reduce costs, eliminate redundancy, and improve access to care for the service member and veteran.

Codify the Quarterly SecDef and SecVA Meetings

There's no question that strong personalities in leadership positions are behind almost all examples of successful collaboration efforts. Strong leaders want to create cultures in their organizations that enable collaboration. They understand that the work of creating this culture starts with them; it requires them to strengthen relationships with other agencies. One such example is the quarterly DoD and VA Secretaries meeting established by Secretary Gates and Secretary Shinseki in 2011. This partnership exists in large part because of the decisive leadership initiative shown by Secretary Gates and

Secretary Shinseki, forging a relationship between the two Departments. The quarterly

meetings provide both Departments a means to look for ways to achieve greater

efficiencies, unity of effort, and practice good governance. For example, the focus

areas discussed during the February 2012 meeting between Secretary of Defense,

Leon Panetta, and VA Secretary Eric Shinseki included: the Disability Evaluation

System, Electronic Health Record, joint Pharmacy initiatives, Transition programs, and

Recovery Care Coordination for the wounded, ill and injured.

The topics discussed reflect a shared purpose and unity of effort between the

Departments. The quarterly meeting provides an opportunity to discuss shared

accomplishments, challenges meet and overcome, and what lessons have been

learned along the way. Although the quarterly meetings have been successful now,

what's to say they will continue with a new administration and new Secretaries? New

teams tend to discard all the previous teams policies and ideas and begin fresh. What if

personalities begin to get in the way and the quarterly meetings cease to exist? A

recommendation to sustain the successful collaboration effort is to immediately codify

the quarterly Secretaries meeting through legislative reform. There is no question that

collaboration will become more prevalent in the future as congress and other

stakeholders seek to reduce duplication, improve efficiency, and decrease spending. A

codified quarterly Secretaries meeting creates a practice of collaboration by two

department Secretaries, and demonstrates their continued effort for cultural change.

Reform Congressional Oversight

As stated earlier, there is no alternative for an involved Congress. They are the

only entity that can squash the bureaucratic chaos that impedes interagency collaboration. Without Congressional oversight, there is little accountability. This leads to delays, budget overruns, and programs that never reach full implementation. Additionally, Congress appropriates funds that put resources behind the programs. Any major initiative or program without the money to execute it is a moot point. Examples such as the Goldwater-Nichols Reform NA of 1986; *Public Law 97-174*, S.266, *Veterans Administration and Department of Defense Health Resources Sharing and Emergency Operations Act* of 1982; *National Defense Authorization Act (NDAA) of FY2004* that created the DoD/VA JEC; and others, tell us that without oversight the interagency collaboration process may never get set in motion.

Just as important as it was to introduce reform for DoD and VA interagency process, it is absolutely critical to implement similar reform in Congress. No single committee in Congress is responsible for the DoD/VA interagency process. Therefore, a recommendation is to mandate congressional membership in both the DoD and VA committees to ensure visibility of critical issues, continuity, and to improve cross-pollination amongst Congress. Currently, dual membership in the House/Senate Veterans' Affairs Committee (HVAC/SVAC) and House/Senate Armed Service Committee (HASC/SASC) is voluntary. In the House of Representatives, there are only four dual-members of both the HVAC (26 total members)[90] and HASC (62 total members).[91] In the Senate, there are five dual-members of both the SVAC (15 total members)[92] and SASC (25 total members).[93] Furthermore, the HVAC/HASC and the SVAC/SASC should hold joint hearings on key issues to ensure effective and efficient oversight of joint programs, policies, and initiatives that cross Departmental boundaries. Lastly, with the current fiscal austerity the budget appropriations committee for DoD and

VA need to be reexamined as they fall within the jurisdiction of two different subcommittees. The DoD health care budget falls under the jurisdiction of the U.S. House Appropriations Subcommittee on Defense. The VA health care budget is under the U.S. House Appropriations Subcommittee on Military Construction, Veterans Affairs, and Related Agencies. One could assume that the appropriations process would lead to a vigilant inspection of the budget from all agencies involved. However, what usually happens is a broad review of the budget request, and ultimate approval. The federal budget is so large and complex that it is almost impossible to systematically review every program and request. Therefore, the Departments establish rapport with the subcommittees which deal with their agency to champion their cause and request.

Reform the Education, Training, and Assignment Process

In the end, relationship building matters most in developing a genuine interagency culture. Unfortunately, while policies within the federal government provide for some interagency exposure, in general, they foster individual professional development with an "agency" specific focus. Interagency policy makers could learn from the U.S. military with respect to building culture through personnel policy reform. The GNA of 1986 ensured the professional development of officers with a successful completion of a joint assignment would receive positive consideration at promotion boards. Further, all officers being considered for promotion to general or admiral are required to receive formal joint training and must complete a joint assignment prior to being considered for such boards. This policy ensures that all senior military leaders, regardless of service affiliation, serves in a joint staff billet thus creating a joint culture. Joint assignments, not temporary liaison or Liaison Officer (LNO) duties, are essential in cultivating a joint culture. These assignments allow individuals to become submerged within the specific culture of each service and their capabilities. These "broadening" assignments enhance unity of effort by building lasting relationships and facilitate interoperability at all levels throughout the organization. During a Congressional hearing, Michele Flournoy stated, "This cross-fertilization across the Military Services created the human and cultural foundation on which increasingly integrated joint military operations have been built over the last 18 years. Jointness began as a change of experience that begat a change of mindset and behavior."[94] A similar policy and program could produce like results for DoD and VA. A recommended policy change would be to mandate all senior DoD and VA leaders working in an interagency billet to receive training in interagency coordination. DoD and VA should establish a three to five day DoD/VA interagency training and education program at initial entry, 5, 10, 15, and 25 year mark for anyone working interagency related issues. The training would not have to be as intensive as the military Joint, Interagency, and Multinational Planner's Course given at the National Defense University but detailed enough to address the cultural aspect and the dynamic challenges confronting interagency coordination.

Additionally, interagency personnel assignments would also enhance a common culture within the agencies. The DoD and VA already have some interagency exchange assignments, primarily within the clinical specialty field. Why not begin assignments that are common to both agencies (i.e. administration, information technology, human resource, etc)? These personnel would share lessons learned and best practices to improve their agency's ability to conduct integrated operations once they return to their parent organization. Furthermore, as is the case within in the military to be considered for promotion to the most senior ranks, these interagency assignments should be considered when selecting a person for a senior position within their parent agency. Michele Flournoy went on to say during her Congressional hearing, "Making promotion to SES (or equivalent) as a professional contingent upon spending 2-3 year rotation in another agency would likely turn the prevailing attitude toward interagency rotations on its head: Rather than being seen as a distraction from, if not a detriment to, advancement in one's home agency."[95] Interagency assignments would build personal relationships, a better understanding of the other agencies' capability, and it would produce future leaders with a broader exposure to lead their organization into the future.

Conclusion

Enhancing cross-cultural collaboration between the DoD and VA is a complex and challenging task. Leadership that projects a clear vision that is significant to the stakeholders within and outside the organization, and an active and committed senior executive team is crucial. Although these conditions form the foundation for a collaborative environment, enhancing collaboration that is widely accepted throughout the agency requires active participation by everyone involved in the process. The DoD and VA have made huge progress in caring for our service members, veterans, and their families, however, more must be done. This paper presents several options to improve efficiency and creating more synergy between the two Departments. The saying of, "because it's always been done that way" is clearly a thing of the past in today's austere operational environment.

Endnotes

[1] Mladen Antonov, "Federal deficit tops $1T for third straight year," *USA Today,* August 11, 2011, http://www.usatoday.com/news/washington/2011-08-10-budget-deficit_n.htm, (accessed November 2, 2011).

[2] U.S. Government Accountability Office, *Recovering Servicemembers: DoD and VA Have Made Progress to Jointly Develop Required Policies but Additional Challenges Remain,* (Washington, DC: U.S. Government Accountability Office, April 29, 2009), 2.

[3] David Nakamura and Ed O'Keefe, "Obama seeks more power to merge agencies, streamline government," *The Washington Post,* January 13, 2012, http://www.washingtonpost.com/politics/obama-to-propose-combining-agencies-to-shrink-federal-government/2012/01/13/gIQAHsLqvP_story.html, (accessed January 14, 2012).

[4] U.S. Joint Chiefs of Staff, *Interagency, Intergovernmental Organization, and Nongovernmental Organization Coordination During Joint Operations Vol I,* Joint publication 3-08 (Washington, DC: U.S. Joint Chiefs of Staff, March 17, 2006), I-6.

[5] U.S. Department of Defense, *About the Department of Defense (DOD),* http://www.defense.gov/about/ (accessed November 30, 2011).

[6] Ibid.

[7] Joint Chiefs of Staff, *About the Joint Chiefs of Staff,* http://www.jcs.mil/page.aspx?id=2 (accessed November 28, 2011).

[8] U.S. Department of Veteran Affairs, *VA History in Brief,* VA Pamphlet 80-97-2 (Washington, DC: U.S. Department of Veterans Affairs, September 1997), 3.

[9] Ibid, 4-6.

[10] Ibid, 4.

[11] Ibid, 7.

[12] Ibid, 8.

[13] Ibid, 12.

[14] Ibid, 22.

[15] Ibid, 26.

[16] Eugene Bardach, *Getting Agencies to Work Together: The Practice and Theory of Managerial Craftsmanship,* (Washington, DC: Brookings Institution Press, 1998, 8.

[17] President Harry Truman, "State of the Union 1947 Address," Washington, DC, January 6, 1947, http://www.let.rug.nl/usa/P/ht33/speeches/ht_1947.htm (accessed December 15, 2011).

[18] Lynne K. Zusman and Neil S. Helfand, "National Security Act of 1947," http://www.enotes.com/national-security-act-1947-reference/national-security-act-1947 (accessed December 11, 2011).

[19] Ibid.

[20] James R. Locher III, "HAS IT WORKED? The Goldwater-Nichols Reorganization Act," *Naval War College Review,* Autumn 2001, 99, http://www.usnwc.edu/getattachment/744b0f7d-4a3f-4473-8a27-c5b444c2ea27/Has-It-Worked--The-Goldwater-Nichols-Reorganizatio (accessed December 20, 2011).

[21] Ibid, 105

[22] Clark A. Murdock and Michele A. Flournoy, *Beyond Goldwater-Nichols: U.S. Government and Defense Reform for a New Strategic Era, Phase II Report,* (Center for Strategic and International Studies, Washington, D.C., July 2005), 16.

[23] Judith A. Miller, "Implementing Change," *Preventive Defense Project,* September 2000, 289, http://belfercenter.ksg.harvard.edu/files/kte_ch11.pdf (accessed November 17, 2011).

[24] National Commission on Terrorist Attacks Upon the United States, "What to Do? A Global Strategy," http://www.9-11commission.gov/report/911Report_Ch12.htm (accessed December 21, 2011).

[25] Tom Davis, *A Failure of Initiative, The Final Report of the Select Bipartisan Committee to Investigate the Preparation and Response to Hurricane Katrina*, Executive Summary (U.S. House of Representatives, Washington, D.C. 20515), xi, http://www.gpoaccess.gov/katrinareport/mainreport.pdf) (accessed December 22, 2011).

[26] *Veterans Administration and Department of Defense Health Resources Sharing and Emergency Operations Act,* Public Law 97-174, 97th Congress, 2nd Session, (January 1, 1982).

[27] TRICARE Management Activity, *DoD/VA Program Coordination,* http://www.tricare.mil/DVPCO/default.cfm (accessed December 2, 2011*).*

[28] *National Defense Authorization Act (NDAA) for FY2004*, Public Law 108-136, Section 583, 108th Congress (November 24, 2003), http://www.dod.gov/dodgc/olc/docs/2004NDAA.pdf (accessed November 20, 2011).

[29] Ibid.

[30] Ibid.

[31] Ibid.

[32] Department of Veterans Affairs and Department of Defense Joint Executive Council, *Joint Strategic Plan Fiscal Years 2011-2013*, (Washington, DC: U.S. Department of Veterans Affairs, September 1997), 5.

[33] John Medve, "VA/DoD Collaboration Overview," briefing slides, Washington, DC: U.S. Department of Veterans Affairs, September 20, 2011.

[34] U.S. Government Accountability Office, *Recovering Servicemembers: DOD and Have Jointly Developed the Majority of Required Policies but Challenges Remain* (Washington, DC: U.S. Government Accountability Office, July 2009), 2.

[35] United States, Presidential Commission on Care for America's Returning Wounded Warriors, *Report to the President,* Washington: The Commission, July 2007.

[36] U.S. Deputy Secretary of Defense Gordon R. England, "Subject: Senior Oversight Committee," memorandum for Secretaries of the Military Departments, Chairman of the Joint Chiefs of Staff, etc, Washington, DC, May 3, 2007.

[37] U.S. Government Accountability Office, *Recovering Servicemembers: DOD and Have Jointly Developed, 2.*

[38] Medve, "VA/DoD Collaboration Overview," briefing slides.

[39] U.S. Secretary of Defense Robert Gates and Acting Secretary of Veterans Affairs, "The role and contribution of the Department of Veterans Affairs (DVA) and Department of Defense (DOD) in the establishment and operation of the Federal Recovery Coordination Program (FRCP) to serve wounded, ill, and injured service members, veterans, and their families," Memorandum of Understanding, Washington, DC, October 30, 2007.

[40] U.S. Government Accountability Office, *DOD and VA Health Care, Action Needed to Strengthen Integration across Care Coordination and Case Management Programs,* (Washington, DC: U.S. Government Accountability Office, October 6, 2011), 3.

[41] U.S. Government Accountability Office, *Recovering Servicemembers: DOD and Have Jointly Developed, 9.*

[41] U.S. Government Accountability Office, *VA and Defense Health Care: Evolving Health Care Systems Require Rethinking of Resource Sharing Strategies* (Washington, DC: U.S. Government Accountability Office, May 2000), 21.

[42] U.S. Government Accountability Office, *DOD and VA Health Care, Action Needed to Strengthen Integration, 3.*

[43] Karen Guice, "Overarching Integrated Product Team" briefing slides, Washington, DC: U.S. Department of Veterans Affairs, December 8, 2010.

[44] *National Defense Authorization Act (NDAA) for FY2008*, Public Law 110-181, Section 1611, 110th Congress (January 28, 2008), http://www.dod.gov/dodgc/olc/docs/pl110-181.pdf (accessed January 5, 2011).

[45] U.S. Government Accountability Office, *DOD and VA Health Care, Action Needed to Strengthen Integration, 4.*

[46] *National Defense Authorization Act (NDAA) for FY2008*, Public Law 110-181, Section 1635.

[47] Ibid.

[48] Nicole Johnson, "DoD, VA renew joint approach to health IT," *Federal Times*, August 12, 2011, http://www.federaltimes.com/article/20110812/IT03/108120302/ (accessed February 2, 2012).

[49] Department of Defense and Department of Veterans Affairs, "Interagency Program Office (IPO) Charter," Washington, DC, October 27, 2011.

[50] U.S. Government Accountability Office, *VA and DOD Health Care: First Federal Health Care Center Established, but Implementation Concerns Need to Be Addressed,* (Washington, DC: U.S. Government Accountability Office, July 2011), 1-2.

[51] Ibid, 1-2.

[52] Ibid, 10.

[53] Alice Lipowicz, "VA, DOD agree on joint platform for e-health records, Shinseki says," March 31, 2011, http://fcw.com/articles/2011/03/31/va-dod-joint-platform-for-ehealth-records.aspx (accessed January 9, 2012).

[54] U.S. Department of Defense Task Force on the Care Management, and Transition of Recovering Wounded, Ill, and Injured Members of the Armed Forces,

2010-2011 Annual Report, (Alexandria, VA: Recovering Warrior Task Force, September 2, 2011), 23-24.

[55] Ibid, 23-24.

[56] Ibid, 23.

[57] John Campbell and John Medve, "SOC-JEC Consolidation Plan Decision Brief," briefing slides, Washington DC: U.S. Department of Veterans Affairs, January 2012.

[58] Ibid.

[59] U.S. Government Accountability Office, *DOD and VA Health Care, Action Needed to Strengthen Integration,* 2.

[60] U.S. Government Accountability Office, *DOD and VA Health Care, Action Needed to Strengthen Integration,* 8.

[61] U.S. Government Accountability Office, *DOD and VA Health Care, Action Needed to Strengthen Integration,* 11.

[62] U.S. Department of the Army, *Army Leadership: Competent, Confident, and Agile,* Army Regulation 6-22 (Washington, DC: U.S. Department of the Army, October 2006), 1-2.

[63] Sunil B. Desai, "Solving the Interagency Puzzle," *Hoover Institution Policy Review,* No. 129, February 1, 2005, http://www.hoover.org/publications/policy-review/article/7108 (accessed December 1, 2011).

[64] John Burdett, *"Wounded Warrior Care and Transition Policy,"* remarks and briefing, Report of the Recovering Warrior Task Force recommendations, Alexandria, VA, February 21, 2012.

[65] Ibid.

[66] U.S. Department of Defense Task Force on the Care Management, and Transition of Recovering Wounded, Ill, and Injured Members, 3.

[67] Jim Garamone, "Pace Proposes Interagency Goldwater-Nichols Act," *American Forces Press Service,* September 7, 2004, http://www.au.af.mil/au/awc/awcgate/dod/n09072004_2004090707.htm (accessed December 11, 2011).

[68] John Medve, "VA/DoD Collaboration Overview," briefing slides, Washington, DC: U.S. Department of Veterans Affairs, September 20, 2011.

[69] Ibid.

[70] U.S. Department of Defense Personnel and Readiness, *Wounded Warrior Care and Transition Policy Mission statement,* http://prhome.defense.gov/WWCTP/Mission.aspx (accessed October 29, 2011).

[71] Karen Jowers, "DoD Slashes Staff in Wounded Warrior Care office," *Army Times,* January 16, 2012, 8-9.

[72] Nick Wakeman, "How Sept 11 changed government contracting forever," *Washington Technology,* September 7, 2011, http://washingtontechnology.com/articles/2011/08/29/cover-sept-11-legacy.aspx (accessed March 1, 2012).

[73] Ron Nixon, "Government Pays More in Contracts, Study Finds,*" The New York Times,"* September 12, 2011, http://www.nytimes.com/2011/09/13/us/13contractor.html (accessed March 9, 2012).

[74] Ibid.

[75] Alice Lipowicz, "VA cancels joint platform contract due to alleged conflict of interest," *Washington Technology,* February 29, 2012, http://fcw.com/articles/2012/02/29/va-cancels-joint-platform-contract-due-to-alleged-conflict-of-interest-report.aspx (accessed March 1, 2012).

[76] U.S. Government Accountability Office, *Electronic Health Record: DoD and VA Should Remove Barriers and Improve Efforts to Meet Their Common System Needs* (Washington, DC: U.S. Government Accountability Office, February 2011), 10.

[77] Ibid.

[78] Bob Brewin, "Gates, Shinseki detail joint health record management and development plans," *Nextgov,* May 26, 2011, http://www.nextgov.com/nextgov/ng_20110526_6089.php (accessed February 2, 2012).

[79] U.S. Department of Defense Personnel and Readiness Information Management (P&R IM), *Virtual Lifetime Electronic Record,* http://www.prim.osd.mil/init/vler.html, (accessed February 5, 2012).

[80] Ibid.

[81] U.S. Government Accountability Office, *Electronic Health Record: DoD and VA Should Remove Barriers,* 10.

[82] Office of Management and Budget, *The Mission and Structure of the Office of Management and Budget,* http://www.whitehouse.gov/omb/organization_mission, (accessed October 12, 2011).

[83] Ibid.

[84] Michele A. Flournoy, "Achieving Unity of Effort in Interagency Operations," Congressional Testimony before the House Armed Service Subcommittee on Oversight and Investigations, January 29, 2008, http://www.google.com/url?q=http://kms1.isn.ethz.ch/serviceengine/Files/ISN/122354/ip ublicationdocument_singledocument/ec849106-fbc2-4bf9-b9d4-950ba79fbc85/en/CNASTestimony_FlournoyHASCJan2908.pdf&sa=U&ei=1SowT4vDH a7H0AG7nvSSCw&ved=0CBAQFjAA&usg=AFQjCNGK05K6xheIbQZ0MPV0pgM5dZtp LQ (accessed November 20, 2011).

[85] Global Security, "History of the Army's Lessons Learned System," *GlobalSecurity.org,* http://www.globalsecurity.org/military/library/report/call/call_97-13_history.htm (accessed February 20, 2012).

[86] Ibid.

[87] Johnson, "DoD, VA renew joint approach to health IT."

[88] U.S. Department of the Army, *Operations,* Army Regulation 3-0 (Washington, DC: U.S. Department of the Army, June 2001), 4-11.

[89] U.S. Congress, Committee on Veterans' Affairs, Subcommittee on Health, *The Federal Recovery Coordination Program: Assessing Progress Toward Improvement,* 112th Cong, 1st sess, October 6, 2011.

[90] *House Committee on Veterans Affairs Home Page,* http://veterans.house.gov/full-committee (accessed March 2, 2012).

[91] *House Armed Services Committee Home Page,* http://armedservices.house.gov/ (accessed March 2, 2012).

[92] *U.S. Senate Committee on Veterans' Affairs Home Page,* http://veterans.senate.gov/ (accessed March 2, 2012).

[93] *U.S. Senate Armed Services Committee Home Page,* http://armed-services.senate.gov/ (accessed March 2, 2012).